[Jesus said
God made male and female to be together.
Because of this, a man leaves father and
mother, and in marriage he becomes
one flesh with a woman—
no longer two individuals, but forming a
new unity."

MARK 10:6–8 THE MESSAGE

O, there is nothing holier, in this life of ours,

than the first consciousness of love

—the first fluttering of its silken wings.

HENRY WADSWORTH LONGFELLOW

_____

Presented to

_____

Presented by

_____

Date

There is no more *lovely*, friendly,
and *charming* relationship, communion,
or company than a good *marriage*.

MARTIN LUTHER

On Your Wedding Day

wishing you a love that lasts forever

SPIRIT PRESS

Marriages are made in *heaven*.

JOHN LYLY

Even if marriages are
made in heaven, husbands and
wives have to be responsible
for the maintenance.

A good marriage is not one where perfection reigns:
it is a relationship where a healthy perspective
overlooks a multitude of "unresolvables."

JAMES DOBSON

Give honor to marriage, and remain faithful
to one another in marriage.

HEBREWS 13:4 NLT

Knit your *hearts* with an unslipping knot.

WILLIAM SHAKESPEARE

Love is patient and kind.
Love is not jealous or boastful or proud or rude.
Love does not demand its own way.

1 CORINTHIANS 13:4–5 NLT

Marrying for love
may be a bit risky,
but it is so honest that God
can't help but smile on it.

JOSH BILLINGS

my love

Come live with me and be my love,

And we will all the pleasures prove

That hills and valleys, dales and fields,

. . .

Or woods or steepy mountain yields.

And I will make thee beds of roses

And a thousand fragrant posies,

A cap of flowers, and a kirtle

Embroider'd all with leaves of myrtle.

CHRISTOPHER MARLOWE

God delights in those who keep their promises.

PROVERBS 12:22 TLB

real love

Love is what you've been through with somebody.

JAMES THURBER

[Jesus said,] "A new commandment I give to you,
that you *love* one another; as I have *loved* you,
that you also *love* one another."

JOHN 13:34 NKJV

Try praising your wife even if it does frighten her at first.

BILLY SUNDAY

Be good husbands to your wives.
Honor them, delight in them.

1 PETER 3:7 THE MESSAGE

You are a *garden* locked up,

my sister, my bride;

you are a *spring* enclosed,

a sealed fountain.

SONG OF SONGS 4:12 NIV

my bride

Chains do not hold a marriage together.

It is threads, hundreds of tiny

threads that sew people

together through the years.

SIMONE SIGNORET

A *perfect* wife is one who doesn't expect
a *perfect* husband.

Wives, understand and support your husbands
in ways that show your support for Christ.

EPHESIANS 5:22 THE MESSAGE

Husband and wife must
delight in the love and company
and lives of each other.
When husband and wife take
pleasure in each other,
it unites them in duty, helps
them with ease to do their work
and bear their burdens,
and is a major part of the
comfort of marriage.

RICHARD BAXTER

Teacher, *tender*, comrade, *wife*.

A fellow-farer true through life.

ROBERT LOUIS STEVENSON

In the *new life* of God's grace, you're equals.

Treat your wives, then, as *equals*

so your prayers don't run aground.

1 PETER 3:7 THE MESSAGE

Wives, understand and support
your husbands by submitting to
them in ways that honor the Master.
Husbands, go all out in love for
your wives. Don't take
advantage of them.

COLOSSIANS 3:18–19 THE MESSAGE

Think not because you now are wed
That all your courtship's at an end.

ANTONIO HURTADO DE MENDOZA

Husbands, love your wives, just as Christ also
loved the church and gave Himself for her.

EPHESIANS 5:25 NKJV

Be happy with your wife and find your joy

with the woman you married—pretty and graceful

as a deer. Let her charms keep you happy;

let her surround you with her love.

PROVERBS 5:18–19 GNT

A good *marriage* is one in which each partner
appoints the other to be the *guardian* of his solitude,
and thus they show each other the greatest possible trust.

RAINER MARIA RILKE

Marriage should be a duet—when one sings,

the other claps.

JOE MURRAY

A wife with strength of character
is the crown of her husband.

PROVERBS 12:4 GOD'S WORD

soul mates

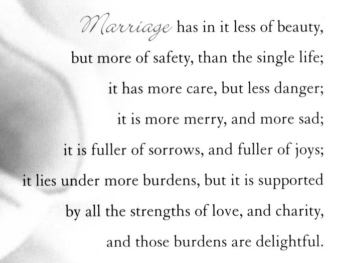

Marriage has in it less of beauty,

but more of safety, than the single life;

it has more care, but less danger;

it is more merry, and more sad;

it is fuller of sorrows, and fuller of joys;

it lies under more burdens, but it is supported

by all the strengths of love, and charity,

and those burdens are delightful.

JEREMY TAYLOR

Successful marriage is always a triangle:
a man, a woman, and God.

CECIL MYERS

He who finds a wife finds a good thing,
and obtains favor from the LORD.

PROVERBS 18:22 NKJV

love never fails

Love . . . bears all things,

believes all things,

hopes all things,

endures all things.

Love never fails.

1 CORINTHIANS 13:4, 7–8 NKJV

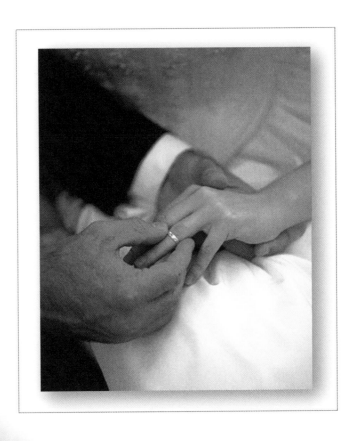

Sweet is the smile of home;

the mutual look,

When *hearts* are of each other sure.

JOHN KEBLE

House and land are handed down from parents,
but a congenial spouse comes straight from GOD.

PROVERBS 19:14 THE MESSAGE

By *wisdom* a house is built,
and through *understanding* it is established;
through *knowledge* its rooms are filled
with rare and beautiful treasures.

PROVERBS 24:3–4 NIV

my treasure

The Bible opens and closes with a *wedding*.

SELWYN HUGHES

Be the mate God designed *you* to be.

ANTHONY T. EVANS

Continue to reverence the Lord all the time,
for surely you have a wonderful
future ahead of you.

PROVERBS 23:17–18 TLB

Grow old along with me!

The best is yet to be,

The last of life, for which the first was made:

Our times are in His hand

Who saith "A whole I planned,

Youth shows but half; trust God:

see all, nor be afraid!"

ROBERT BROWNING

forever my love

On Your Wedding Day
ISBN 1-40372-027-4

Published in 2006 by Spirit Press, an imprint of Dalmatian Press, LLC.
Copyright © 2006 Dalmatian Press, LLC. Franklin, Tennessee 37067.

Editor: Lila Empson
Compiler: Snapdragon Editorial Group, Inc., Tulsa, Oklahoma
Design: Diane Whisner, Tulsa, Oklahoma

Printed in China

14946

06 07 08 09 LPU 10 9 8 7 6 5 4 3 2 1